RUGBY

Penguin Random House

Senior editor Satu Hämeenaho-Fox
Senior art editor Fiona Macdonald
Design assistant Xiao Lin
Project art editors Jaileen Kaur, Nehal Verma
DTP designer Syed Mohammad Farhan
Sr DTP designers Jagtar Singh, Dheeraj Singh
Jacket designer Elle Ward
Managing editor Laura Gilbert
Managing art editor Diane Peyton Jones
Senior producer Tony Phipps
Picture researcher Aditya Katyal
Creative director Helen Senior
Publisher Sarah Larter

Fact-checker Richard Mead

Written, designed, edited, and
project-managed
for DK by Dynamo Ltd.

First published in Great Britain in 2019 by
Dorling Kindersley Limited
80 Strand, London, WC2R 0RL

Copyright © 2019 Dorling Kindersley Limited
A Penguin Random House Company
10 9 8 7 6 5 4 3 2 1
001–314175–Aug/2019

A CIP catalogue record for this book
is available from the British Library.
ISBN: 978-0-2413-7932-5

Printed and bound in China

A WORLD OF IDEAS:
SEE ALL THERE IS TO KNOW

www.dk.com

HELLO!

Welcome to your one-stop guide to everything rugby! It's packed with all you need to know from the Six Nations to the Rugby World Cup. This book covers tag, touch, and even snow rugby, and it's filled with top tips, fun facts, and famous faces. You'll get to explore the fascinating history of the game while discovering its legendary players, old and new.

CONTENTS

WHAT IS RUGBY?

Rugby is a team sport that has existed for nearly 200 years. There are many forms of the game and they all have slightly different rules. Let's get to grips with the basics.

AIM OF THE GAME

The aim in a rugby match is always the same: to use the ball to score more points than the other team.

THE PITCH

The maximum size of a rugby pitch is 144 m (157 yds) long and 70 m (77 yds) wide. The two goal lines are 100 m (109 yds) apart and the rest of the pitch is made up of the two goal areas.

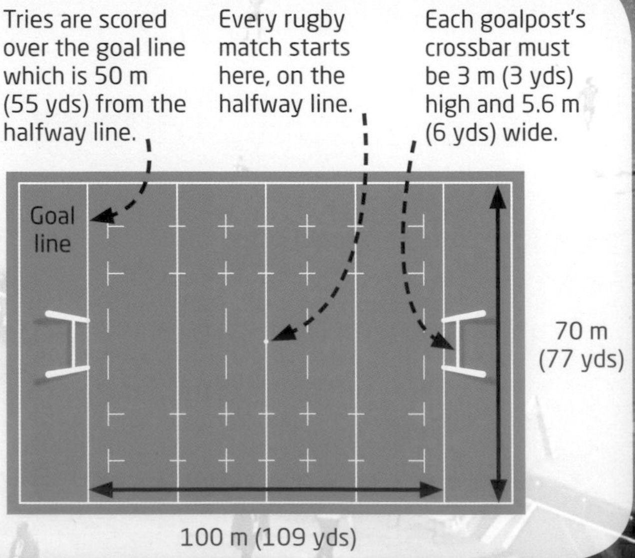

Tries are scored over the goal line which is 50 m (55 yds) from the halfway line.

Every rugby match starts here, on the halfway line.

Each goalpost's crossbar must be 3 m (3 yds) high and 5.6 m (6 yds) wide.

Goal line

70 m (77 yds)

100 m (109 yds)

4

THE BALL

The rugby ball is oval-shaped and it can be kicked, carried, or passed from player to player. Find out about variations in the ball's shape and size on page 17.

Words to know

Lineout

The ball is thrown (often by the hooker) to restart play after it's gone into touch (gone out of the playing area). Both team's forwards will then compete to win possession of the ball.

Try

A player takes hold of the ball and grounds it (touches it to the ground), on or over the goal line. A try scores five points for the team.

Conversion

A team that scores a try gets a free kick at goal. The aim is to kick the ball over the crossbar between the posts, earning two points.

Offside

A player must not gain an advantage by being in front of the ball when it is passed. If they do, the referee will award a penalty to the other team.

Knock-on pass

The ball can only be thrown sideways or backwards. Referees will award a foul against a team if the ball gets knocked forward.

PLAY TO WIN

While players are doing their best to overcome their opponents and score points, the referee has to make sure they don't break any rules, and punish players who do.

80 MINUTES

Each match is played over 40-minute halves with a maximum 10-minute break in the middle.

KICKING SKILLS

To score points from a conversion, drop goal, or penalty kick, players must be very accurate. The ball has to fly in between the goal posts and over the crossbar.

POINTS

To win a match, a team must score points. Players can score points with a try (five points), a conversion (two points), a penalty kick, or a drop goal (three points each).

SUBSTITUTES

A Rugby Union team is made up of 15 players and eight substitutes. All eight substitutes can be brought on during a game to replace tired or injured players.

PENALTIES

The referee can award a penalty when a foul is committed. A kick to touch, kick at goal, scrum, and tap are all types of penalty. The referee chooses one of these to restart the game.

Cards

Yellow or red cards are also given for fouls. A player shown a yellow card must leave the pitch for 10 minutes. For more serious fouls, a red card is shown and the player can no longer play in that game.

RUGBY HISTORY

Rugby has been played for hundreds of years, and no one is completely sure who first invented it. Since the 19th century, it has evolved into a professional sport watched by millions.

PICKING UP THE BALL

William Webb Ellis, a 16-year-old pupil at Rugby School in Warwickshire, UK, is playing football when he picks up the ball and runs with it in his arms. Although many question whether this story is true, the World Cup winner's trophy is named the Webb Ellis Cup.

William Webb Ellis as an adult

1823

1907

1870

1895

England Rugby Union Team, c. March 1871.

THE RFU IS BORN

Players Edwin Ash and Benjamin Burns write to *The Times* newspaper suggesting that rugby needs a code of practice. A year later, 21 clubs meet in London and create English Rugby's governing body, known as the Rugby Football Union (RFU).

THE SPLIT

Major clubs from the counties of Lancashire and Yorkshire hold a meeting at a hotel in Huddersfield, UK. As a result, 22 clubs split from the Rugby Football Union to form the Northern Rugby Football Union.

DOWN UNDER

In 1907, a politician called Henry Hoyle organizes a meeting to form the New South Wales Rugby Football League. He is elected its first president. In 1924, the organization works with the Queensland Rugby League to set up the Australian Rugby League.

GLOBAL GAME

The first World Cup is played in Australia and New Zealand by 16 nations. Hosts New Zealand win the cup. The tournament has been held every four years since. The World Cup is run by the sport's international governing body, World Rugby.

RENAMED

The Northern Rugby Football Union changes its name and becomes the Rugby Football League.

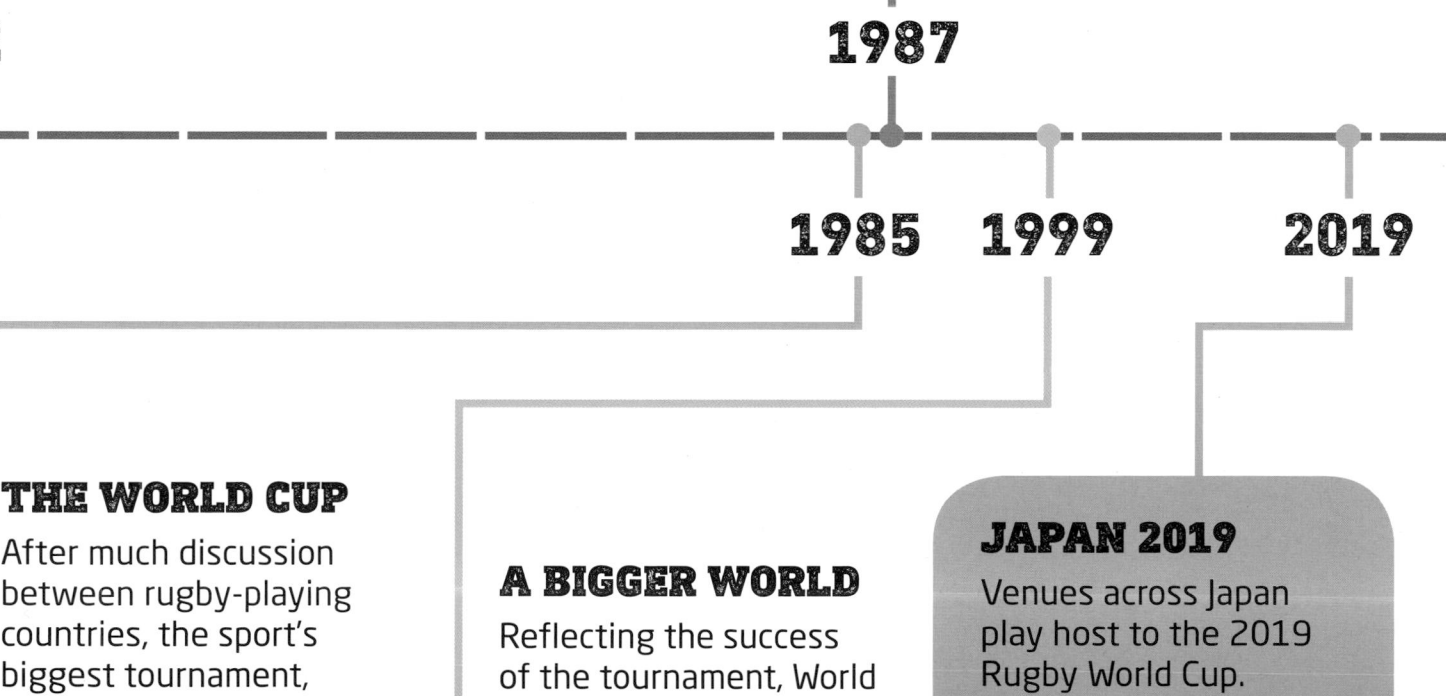

1922

1987

1985   **1999**   **2019**

THE WORLD CUP

After much discussion between rugby-playing countries, the sport's biggest tournament, and its first global competition, is created.

A BIGGER WORLD

Reflecting the success of the tournament, World Cup participation grows to 20 countries.

JAPAN 2019

Venues across Japan play host to the 2019 Rugby World Cup.

FORMS OF RUGBY

There are many different ways to play rugby and each has a unique set of rules. There are also variants depending on different ages and abilities. Rugby can be played on different surfaces, from grass to snow.

UNION AND LEAGUE RULES

- ★ The aim is to score more points than the other team.
- ★ A game is started by a kick from the halfway line.
- ★ A game is played over 80 minutes (in two halves of 40 minutes each).
- ★ A player can run with the ball, kick it, and pass it.
- ★ A player cannot pass the ball forwards.
- ★ A player can tackle an opponent to get the ball.
- ★ A team of officials will take charge of the game.
- ★ A team scores points with a try, conversion, or a kick at goal.

UNION

The most popular form of the game with more than three million players worldwide.

LEAGUE

Rugby league is a faster game than union, which it split from in 1895. There are key differences in the rules.

RULE DIFFERENCES

* ★ 15 players
* ★ 8 substitutes
* ★ 3 officials
* ★ No limit on tackles
* ★ 5 points for a try
* ★ There are lineouts, rucks, and mauls. Learn about these on pages 32-33.

* ★ 13 players
* ★ 4 substitutes
* ★ 4 officials
* ★ 6 tackle limit
* ★ 4 points for a try
* ★ There are no lineouts or mauls. Rucks in league differ to union.

WHEELCHAIR RUGBY

This indoor, four-a-side variant of the game is for people who use a wheelchair. Wheelchair rugby is played over four eight-minute quarters and is a popular sport at the Paralympic Games. Players use special, extra-strong wheelchairs. The sport is so rough that it's known as "murderball"!

BEACH RUGBY

Beach rugby is played on sand, with four or seven players on each side. Matches are played on a smaller pitch than union or league, and are split into five- or seven-minute halves.

SNOW RUGBY

The rules of snow rugby are similar to union, but the kit is adapted for snowy conditions and includes leggings and vests. It is vital that players stay warm. Two teams of seven compete over two-, five-, or seven-minute halves in the snow, making snow rugby a fast and exciting game.

SEVENS RUGBY

Sevens is a seven-a-side version of union. A sevens match is split into two seven-minute halves. It is also the form of rugby played at the Olympic Games.

TAG RUGBY

Tag is five- to seven-a-side non-contact rugby. A match is made up of 20-minute halves. Each player wears two tags on their belt. Instead of tackling, defenders must remove a tag from the ball carrier. When a player's tag is removed, they place the ball on the ground and roll it backwards with their foot. If a team is tagged six times in a row, the ball goes to the other team.

GOTCHA!

When a player removes a tag from an opponent, they shout "tag!".

TOUCH RUGBY

Touch rugby is six-a-side, and there is no tackling or kicking. Play starts and restarts at the centre by tapping the ball on the ground. Instead of tackling each other, the defending players touch the ball or the carrier with their hands. When the attacking team is touched, they must place the ball on the ground and step over it. If the attacking team is touched six times, the ball goes to the other team.

MINI RUGBY

Mini rugby is a simple version of rugby union designed to introduce the sport to children under the age of 13. It is played with a smaller ball and on a smaller pitch. The sizes depend on the age group – for example, under-sevens play on a pitch no larger than 60 m by 30 m (66 yds by 33 yds). Team numbers can vary from five to 13 players.

REGULATIONS

Regulations are the set of rules used to control and manage everything to do with a sport. They are enforced by the referee, who knows them off by heart.

The referee blows a whistle to stop and restart play.

REFEREE

A referee is responsible for making sure that everyone follows the rules in a game. They must treat each side fairly and their word is final.

BALL SIZE AND WEIGHT

The rugby ball is oval-shaped, which helps to make passing easier than with a round ball. Rugby union balls are slightly longer than those used in rugby league. League balls tend to be a little fatter and more pointed.

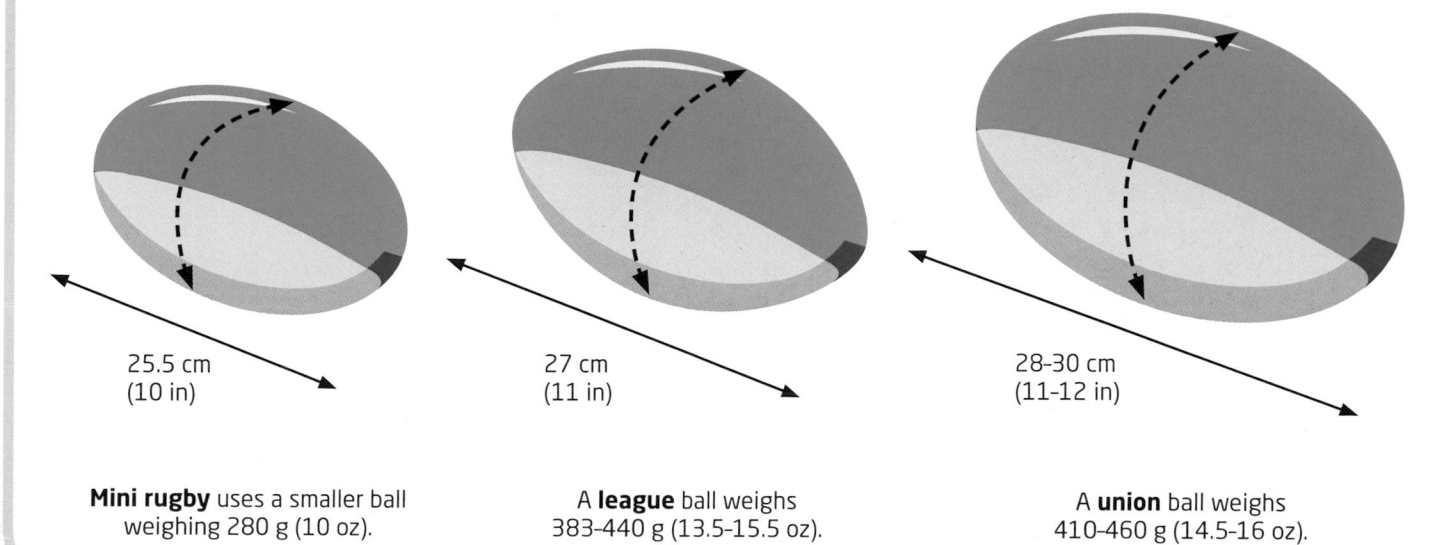

25.5 cm
(10 in)

27 cm
(11 in)

28-30 cm
(11-12 in)

Mini rugby uses a smaller ball weighing 280 g (10 oz).

A **league** ball weighs 383-440 g (13.5-15.5 oz).

A **union** ball weighs 410-460 g (14.5-16 oz).

KIT REGULATIONS

- Players all wear their team's shirt.
- Rugby shorts are made of thick cotton.
- Players can wear mouthguards or gum shields to help protect their teeth.
- Women may wear chest pads and long tights.
- Players cannot wear anything sharp that could cause injury to other players.
- Rugby boots can be studded or bladed. They are heavier than football boots to protect them during rucks and mauls.
- Headguards or padded scrumcaps are advised.
- Shoulder pads and shin guards can be worn.
- ★ Players can wear fingerless gloves.

Dos and don'ts

Here are a few important things to remember when you play rugby.

★ **Tackling:** Players must never tackle an opponent whose feet are off the ground. You can only tackle the ball carrier.

★ **Passing:** You can pass or kick the ball, and you can run with it. Passing the ball forwards is not allowed.

★ **Foul play:** Showing aggression or deliberately causing harm to another player is not allowed.

POSITIONS AND ROLES

In a game of rugby union each team has 15 players. There are eight forwards and seven backs. All of these positions have different roles to play in the game and suit players of all shapes and sizes.

CHOOSE A POSITION

Before starting a game, decide what position you'd like to play. Test out different positions to find out which you like best.

Forward

The forwards are the props, hooker, locks, flankers, and number 8. They tend to be big and heavy. They wear the shirts numbered 1–8.

Back

The backs are the scrum-half, fly-half, wings, centres, and full-back. They tend to be smaller and faster. They wear the shirts numbered 9–15.

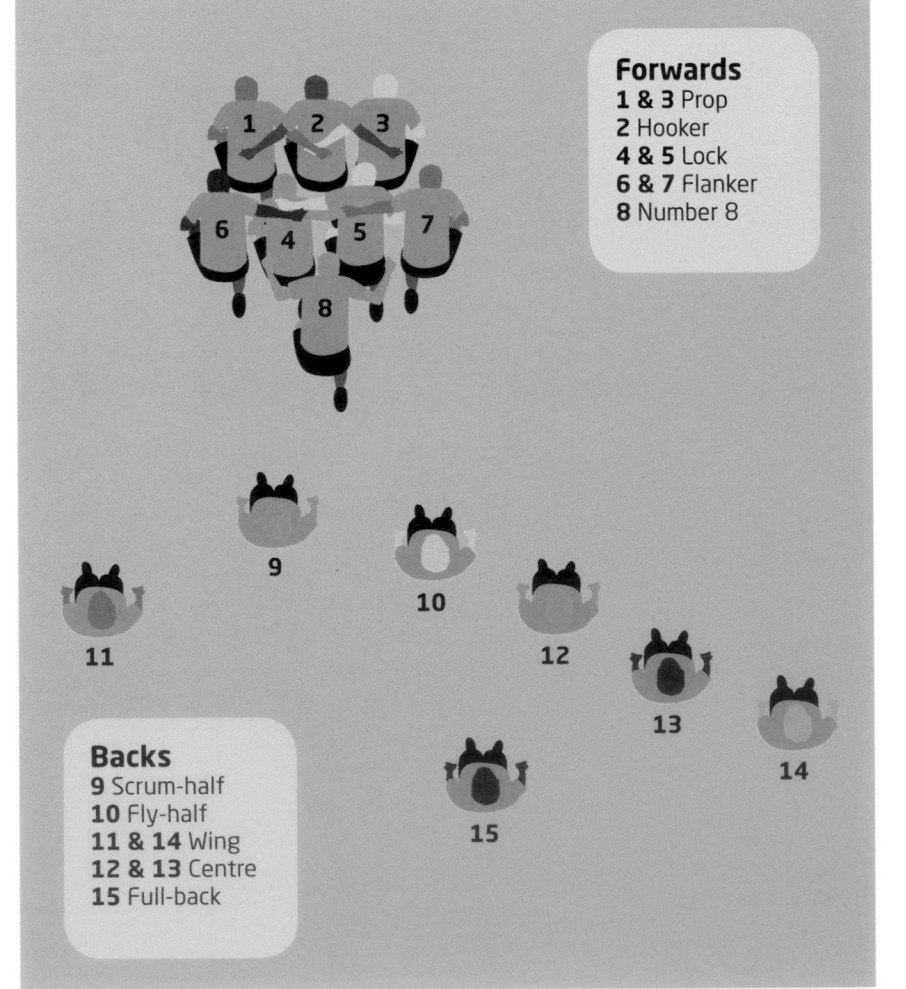

Forwards
1 & 3 Prop
2 Hooker
4 & 5 Lock
6 & 7 Flanker
8 Number 8

Backs
9 Scrum-half
10 Fly-half
11 & 14 Wing
12 & 13 Centre
15 Full-back

HOOKER

Hookers wear a number 2 shirt. In scrums, they play in the front row and try to win the ball by "hooking" it back with their foot.

★ **Agility:** They help to win the ball when under pressure in a scrum, ruck, or maul.

★ **Handling:** They carry the ball towards the opponent's goal line.

★ **Accuracy:** They throw the ball from a lineout. Lineouts restart play when the ball goes into touch (off the field of play at the side).

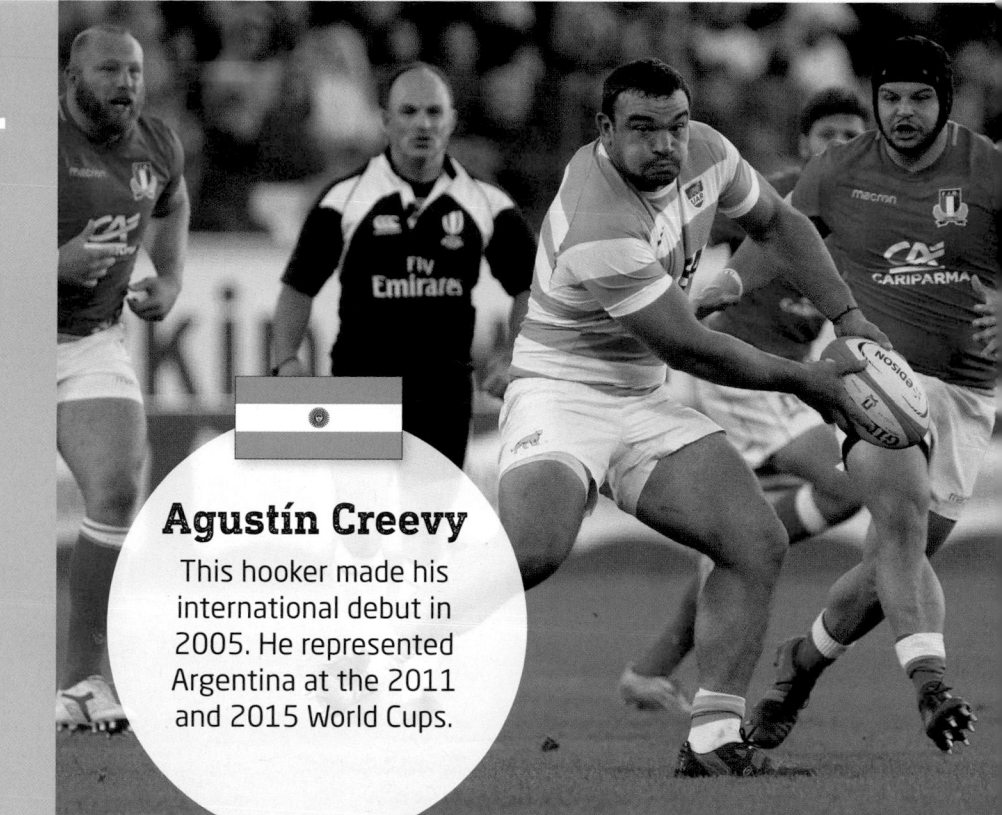

Agustín Creevy

This hooker made his international debut in 2005. He represented Argentina at the 2011 and 2015 World Cups.

PROP

There are two props in a rugby team, who wear the number 1 and 3 shirts. They are usually the strongest players and help in defence and attack.

★ **Strength:** They lift the lock in a lineout and overpower opponents in scrums.

★ **Handling:** They carry the ball forwards for the team.

★ **Tackling:** They stop attacks and win possession of the ball.

Manasa Saulo

This mega-powerful Fijian helped his country to win Pacific Nations Cups in 2015, 2017, and 2018.

LOCK

There are two locks in a rugby team, who wear the number 4 and 5 shirts. They are usually the tallest players and are known as the team's "engine room".

★ **Strength:** They help the team in scrums, rucks, and mauls.

★ **Catching:** They catch and hold onto the ball in a lineout.

★ **Tackling:** They stop attacks and win back possession of the ball.

Maro Itoje

This lock played a starring role at the 2016 Six Nations Championship, which England won. Itoje was also a key member of the 2017 British and Irish Lions squad.

Michael Hooper

This flanker was named Australia's best player in 2013 and 2016. He became Australia's captain in 2017.

FLANKER

There are two flankers in a rugby team, who wear the number 6 and 7 shirts. They are often the fastest players and compete for the ball in rucks.

★ **Fitness:** They need lots of energy to compete in every minute of a game.

★ **Strength:** They help the team in rucks, mauls, and scrums.

★ **Tackling:** They stop attacks and win possession of the ball.

NUMBER 8

Unsurprisingly, a team's number 8 wears the number 8 shirt! They are expected to carry the ball through the opposition and help with defending.

★ **Handling:** They carry the ball and create chances for the team.

★ **Positioning:** They must always stay near the player with the ball.

★ **Tackling:** They stop attacks and win possession of the ball.

Kieran Read

This All Blacks captain made his international debut in 2008. He is now a legend after helping New Zealand win two World Cups, in 2011 and 2015.

SCRUM-HALF

A scrum-half wears the number 9 shirt. They are the key link between the forwards and backs on the pitch.

★ **Handling:** They accurately feed the ball into the scrum and collect it on its return.

★ **Passing:** They quickly start attacks once they get the ball from the scrum.

★ **Speed of thought:** They can make the correct decision before getting possession of the ball.

Morgan Parra

This French star is known as "Le Petit Général", which means "The Little General". Parra helped his country to a Six Nations Grand Slam victory in 2010.

Finn Russell

The Scottish fly-half has been a key player for his country since his debut in 2014. At the 2015 World Cup, he scored a try in Scotland's opening game.

FLY-HALF

The fly-half wears the number 10 shirt. They are the goal-kicker and they also control the speed of the game for their team.

★ **Kicking:** They accurately kick the ball from hand and from the tee (the little stand the ball is placed on), for conversions and penalties.

★ **Vision:** They spot danger and attacking opportunities early.

★ **Leadership:** They make decisions to change the direction of a match.

CENTRE

Each team has an inside centre (number 12) and an outside centre (number 13).

★ **Movement:** They run into space, side-step, and swerve to open up play for their teammates.

★ **Distribution:** They use both kicking and passing skills to direct attacks.

★ **Tackling:** They stop the opposition's backline from advancing towards the try line when they have the ball.

Damian de Allende

The South African has been his country's regular inside centre since 2014. He helped the Springboks finish third at the 2015 Rugby World Cup.

FULL-BACK

The full-back (number 15) is the team's last line of defence. They are also expected to assist in attacking.

★ **Catching:** They receive high kicks while under pressure from opponents.

★ **Kicking:** They accurately kick the ball a long distance away from danger.

★ **Speed:** They join the backline and help in counter-attacks.

Leigh Halfpenny

This Welshman scored 49 out of 79 points for the British and Irish Lions in their 2013 tour of Australia. He helped Wales win the 2012 and 2013 Six Nations.

Jacob Stockdale

This winger scored the equal-highest number of tries (seven) ever in a Six Nations. He was named Player of the Championship after Ireland won a Grand Slam in the 2018 Six Nations.

WING

Each team has a left wing (number 11) and a right wing (number 14). These are often the fastest players and the main try scorers.

★ **Kicking:** They kick the ball from both hand and tee.

★ **Vision:** They spot danger and any attacking opportunities early.

★ **Leadership:** They make big decisions that change and shape the course of a match.

PAST LEGENDS

Players who can score points and lead the team can change the direction of a game or even a tournament. The men's and women's World Cups have showcased some of the best players on the planet.

 **Jonah Lomu**

Lomu was the top try scorer at the two World Cups he played in. He scored four tries in an epic 1995 semi-final performance against England. Unfortunately, he didn't win the trophy as New Zealand finished second in 1995 and fourth in 1999.

TEAM	New Zealand
POSITION	Wing
YEARS	1995, 1999
TRIES	15
POINTS	75

Jonny Wilkinson

In 2003, Wilkinson kicked a World Cup-winning drop-goal in extra time against hosts Australia. After playing in four tournaments, he is the leading points scorer with 277.

TEAM	England
POSITION	Fly-half
YEARS	1999, 2003 (won), 2007, 2011
TRIES	1
POINTS	277

Katherine Merchant

This right wing helped England reach the 2010 final. Merchant lifted the trophy again in 2014. She scored six tries across the two tournaments.

TEAM	England
POSITION	Wing
YEARS	2010, 2014 (won)
TRIES	6
POINTS	30

HOW TO PLAY

To start playing rugby, it's important to learn the game's core skills. Although running is important, the sport is mostly played with the hands. Here are some basic passing, catching, and carrying techniques.

HOW TO PASS

Passing is one of rugby's key techniques. Players must be able to make a pass the right way to give the ball to a teammate. Good passing will get a team up the field and towards the goal quickly. This will present more opportunities to score points and win the match.

Simple pass

Follow these tips to master a simple pass. The aim is to pass the ball to the space your teammate is moving into, rather than simply aiming it at them.

1

Hold the ball with both hands and use your fingers to control it. Keep your head up and look for a teammate to pass to.

2

Swing your arms in the direction of the teammate you want to pass to. Use the hand furthest from the target to push the ball, and the other hand as a guide.

3

Flick your fingers and wrists after you release the ball. This will point your fingers towards the target.

Spin pass

When you have mastered the simple pass, try a spin pass. This is a harder skill, but the ball will fly more accurately over longer distances.

1

Grip the back third of the ball by your hip.

2

Turn your wrist to spin the ball as you release it.

3

Throw your arm forwards, straight at your target.

4

Your elbow should be pointing down.

Ball dynamics

As the ball travels through the air, it experiences four basic forces.

Lift keeps the ball in the air.

The player throwing the ball creates **thrust**.

Drag slows the ball's movement in the air.

Rugby ball

Ball is thrown in this direction.

Gravity pulls the ball towards the ground.

HOW TO CATCH

Catching is a key skill in rugby as the ball has to be passed between players and not kicked. Dropping the ball is risky as the opposing team will probably swoop in and grab it. Here's how to keep the ball safely in your hands.

Simple catch

It's important for a player to be ready to receive a pass at any time. Here's a quick starter's guide to catching a rugby ball.

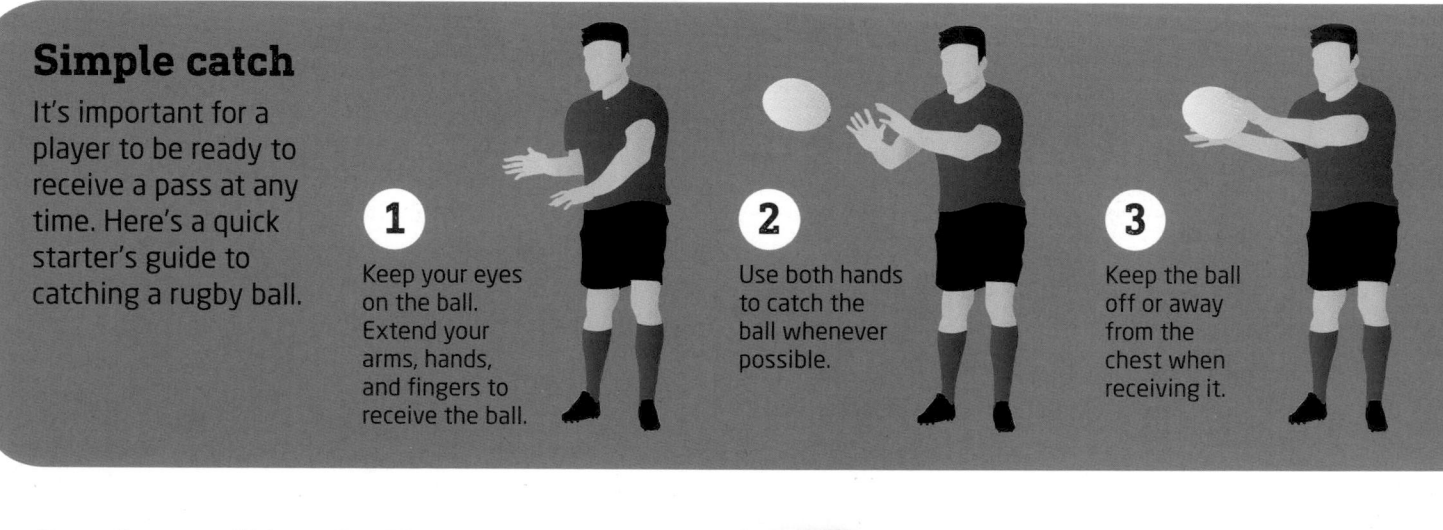

1 Keep your eyes on the ball. Extend your arms, hands, and fingers to receive the ball.

2 Use both hands to catch the ball whenever possible.

3 Keep the ball off or away from the chest when receiving it.

Catch a rolling ball

Catching a rolling, bouncing rugby ball can be tricky, especially in wet conditions. Here's how to keep control of a rolling ball.

Keep your eyes on the ball.

Bend your knees.

Keep your body behind the ball.

Reach with both hands and pick it up.

Catch a high ball

Catching a ball that's been thrown high is difficult, especially if the opposition is close by. Jump high and catch accurately to win the ball.

1

Get in line with the path of the ball. Be sure to keep your eyes on it at all times.

2

Extend your arms towards the ball and bend your elbows. Keep your body side-on to your opponent, and bring one knee up to your waist.

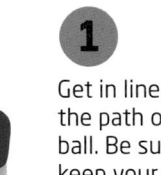

3

Catch the ball above eye level, and bring it in to your body as you land on your feet.

HOW TO HOLD AND CARRY

When playing rugby, it's important to have complete control of the ball as you move around the pitch with it. Here's a guide to carrying the ball securely, and keeping it away from your opponent.

Two-hand carry

Use this when you're not carrying the ball at top speed. Place all of your fingers along the seams at the bottom. Put each thumb on the seams at the top to make a cage-like shape. Hold it firmly out in front of you.

One-hand carry

Use this when you want to run fast and carry the ball at top speed without the risk of dropping it. Grip the ball tightly so that it's between your upper arm and chest. Only the top of the ball should be visible.

PHASES OF PLAY

A rugby match includes many different phases of play that involve different skills. There are four that you'll need to know and master: mauls, rucks, scrums, and lineouts. The referee decides which one will be used to get the game going again.

Scrum

A scrum is used to restart play after a minor rule is broken. Scrums will also be set up if the ball becomes unplayable in a ruck or maul. The forwards push against each other to try and win ground. The scrum half throws the ball into the scrum and the forwards battle it out to gain possession.

1
Before engagement: get on your toes, lean forwards, and keep your head up.

2
On engagement: bend at your hips, keep your hips above your knees, and stay on the balls of your feet.

Maul

A maul happens when the player with the ball is held back by an opponent and then a teammate joins in. It is a way to keep control of the ball and move it towards the opposition's in-goal area. To be called a maul, the ball must not touch the ground.

The ball carrier's teammate holds on.

An opponent also holds the player with the ball.

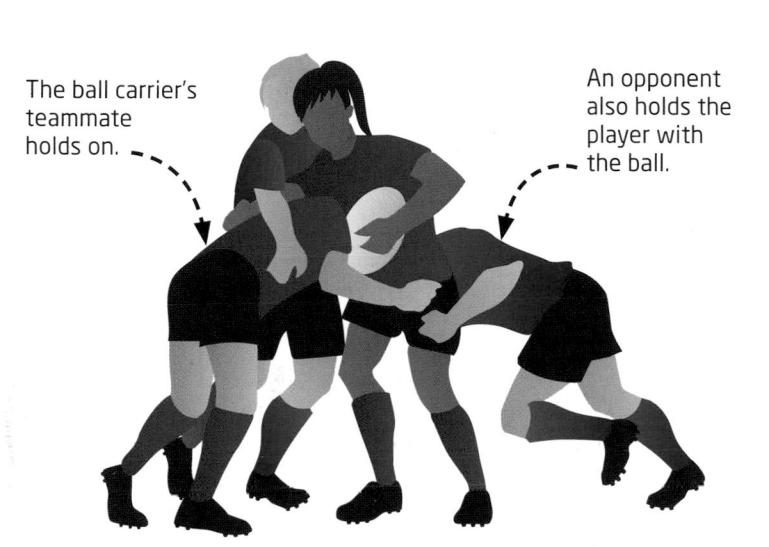

Ruck

In a ruck, players compete to get at the ball when it is on the ground. One or more players from each team must be on their feet and near the ball. Players must not handle the ball in the ruck. Instead they must hook it back with their feet or push the opposition off the ball.

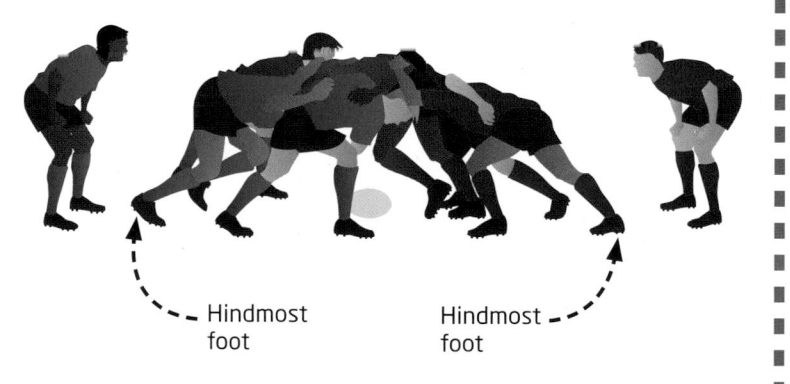

Hindmost foot

Hindmost foot

The ball can only be picked up once it emerges at the team's hindmost (furthest back) foot.

Lineouts

A lineout restarts play when the ball has gone into touch. Each team's forwards line up next to each other and the hooker throws the ball in. One of the forwards is lifted to try and catch the ball in the air. Both team's forwards compete for possession. A minimum of two players from each team are required in a lineout.

PAST LEGENDS

Great players blend the techniques of carrying and passing seamlessly to advance towards the in-goal area. Across a whole tournament, a player must pass the ball hundreds of times.

Sébastien Chabal

The unmistakable bearded Frenchman was part of Les Bleus' (France's national team) squad at the 2003 and 2007 World Cups. At both tournaments, the team lost in the semi-finals against England. The first time was in Australia, the second time on home soil in Paris.

TEAM	France
POSITION	Number 8 / Lock
YEARS	2003, 2007
BORN	December 8, 1977
FROM	Valence, France

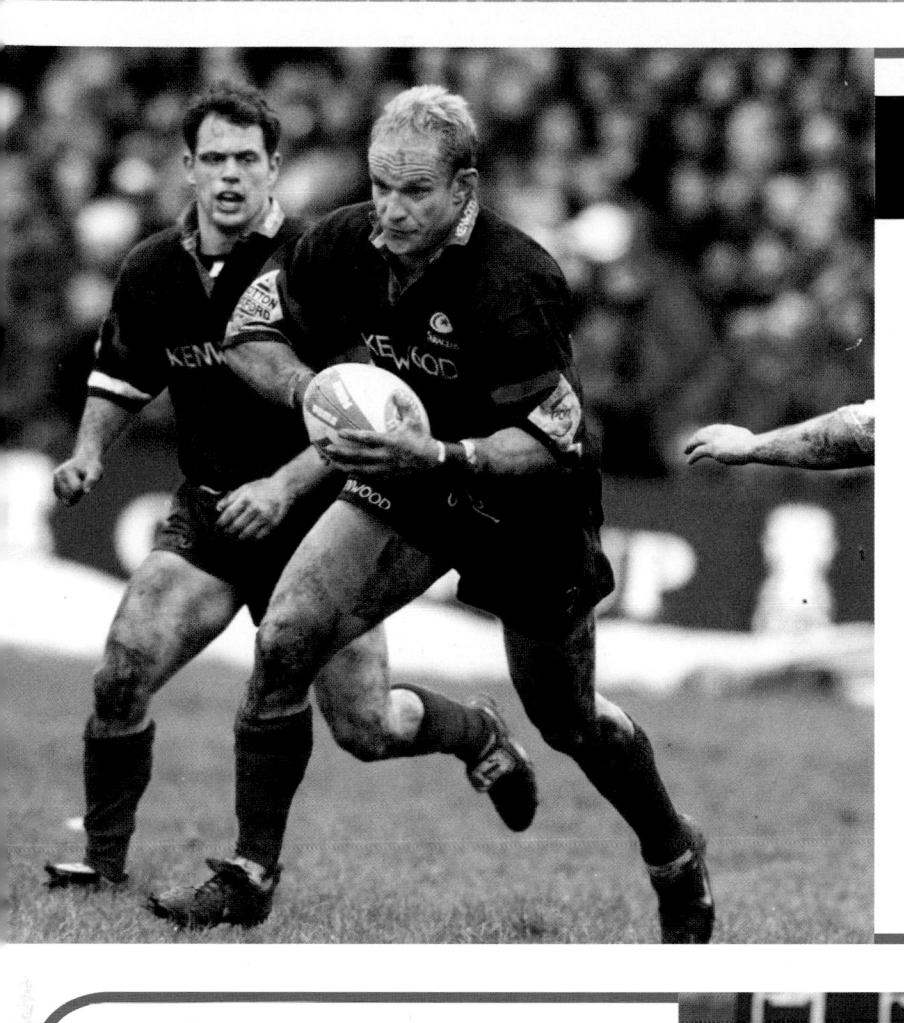

 **Francois Pienaar**

The 1995 South Africa captain took part in one of the tournament's most iconic moments when he received the World Cup trophy from his country's president, Nelson Mandela.

TEAM	South Africa
POSITION	Flanker
YEARS	1995
BORN	January 1, 1967
FROM	Vereeniging, South Africa

 **Anna Richards**

This fly-half won the World Cup four times in a row from 1998 to 2010 with New Zealand's women's team, the Black Ferns.

TEAM	New Zealand
POSITION	Fly-half
YEARS	1991, 1998, 2002, 2006, 2010
BORN	December 3, 1964
FROM	Timaru, New Zealand

HISTORY OF THE WORLD CUP

The men's Rugby World Cup started in 1987 when it was hosted by Australia and New Zealand. The tournament has been packed with magical moments ever since!

HOW IT WORKS

Twenty nations are seeded (given a world ranking) and split into four groups of five. The teams in each group then play each other once, and the top two go through to the quarter-finals. Next, the remaining eight teams play straight knockout matches, and the last nation standing is crowned the world champion.

First ever World Cup

The Rugby Unions of Australia and New Zealand wanted the World Cup to be a global competition for the sport. They shared this idea with other nations and it was accepted in 1985. There were 16 nations in the first ever World Cup, held in May and June 1987.

ROLL OF HONOUR

★ **1987**
  Winner - New Zealand
  Hosts - Australia & New Zealand

★ **1991**
  Winner - Australia
  Hosts - Europe

★ **1995**
  Winner - South Africa
  Hosts - South Africa

★ **1999**
  Winner - Australia
  Hosts - Wales

★ **2003**
  Winner - England
  Hosts - Australia

★ **2007**
  Winner - South Africa
  Hosts - France

★ **2011**
  Winner - New Zealand
  Hosts - New Zealand

★ **2015**
  Winner - New Zealand
  Hosts - England

JAPAN 2019

The ninth men's Rugby World Cup will be hosted in Asia for the first time. Japan defeated Italy and South Africa to be named the hosts.

JAPAN AT THE RWC

Japan have competed in every Rugby World Cup. Their best performance to date was in 2015 when they won three of their games.

TEAMS

- Ireland
- Scotland
- Japan
- Russia
- Samoa
- ★ New Zealand
- South Africa
- Italy
- ★ Namibia
- Canada
- England
- France
- Argentina
- ★ United States
- ★ Tonga
- Australia
- Wales
- Georgia
- Fiji
- Uruguay

20 TEAMS

Where?

The tournament will take place from 20 September to 2 November, 2019. It will be played across 12 venues.

Tokyo

STADIUM STATS

★ The International Stadium (also known as the Nissan Stadium) in Yokohama will host the final match on 2 November, 2019.

★ The International Stadium has room for 72,367 spectators, making it the biggest venue in the tournament.

★ It opened in March 1998 and cost about £495 million to build.

★ The stadium has hosted a variety of music and sporting events, including the 2002 football World Cup final.

International Stadium, Yokohama

SQUAD SIZE

31

The head coach of each squad will select 31 players to take to the tournament.

WORLD CUP IN NUMBERS

Discover fun facts about the men's Rugby World Cup, from the youngest participant to the most tries in a match, tournament, and in the history of the event.

277
MOST WORLD CUP POINTS EVER
Jonny Wilkinson
(England)

126
MOST POINTS IN A TOURNAMENT
Grant Fox
(New Zealand, 1987)

45
MOST POINTS IN ONE MATCH
Simon Culhane
(New Zealand vs Japan, 1995)

WOMEN'S 2017 WORLD CUP

The 2017 Women's Rugby World Cup in Ireland was the biggest WRWC yet. **45,412** fans flocked to the stadiums to watch the games, setting a new attendance record. In the UK, **2.65 million** people watched the final between England and New Zealand on TV.

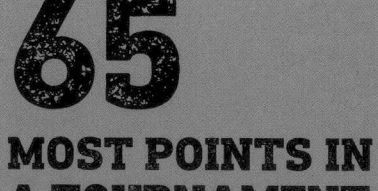

65
MOST POINTS IN A TOURNAMENT
Portia Woodman
(New Zealand)

MOST WORLD CUP TRIES IN TOTAL
15

Bryan Habana (South Africa)
Jonah Lomu (New Zealand)

MOST TRIES IN ONE MATCH
6

Marc Ellis
(New Zealand v Japan, 1995)

MOST DROP GOALS IN ONE MATCH
5

Jannie de Beer
(South Africa v England, 1999)

MOST CONVERSIONS IN A TOURNAMENT
30

Grant Fox
(New Zealand, 1987)

MOST PENALTIES IN A TOURNAMENT
31

Gonzalo Quesada
(Argentina, 1999)

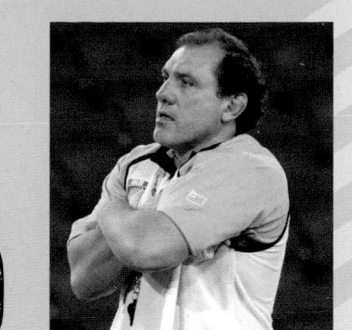

40

OLDEST PLAYER 40 YEARS, 26 DAYS

Diego Ormaechea in 1999
(Uruguay)

18

YOUNGEST PLAYER 18 YEARS, 340 DAYS

Vasil Lobzhanidze in 2015
(Georgia)

117

MOST PLAYER TACKLES

Maria Ribera
(Spain)

299

MOST TEAM POINTS

New Zealand

49

MOST TEAM TRIES

New Zealand

1,002

MOST TEAM TACKLES

Japan

All Women's World Cup stats are from 2017 only as this is the only WRWC for which reliable data is available.

England

England play their home matches at Twickenham near London. They have won the tournament 38 times, with 10 shared victories. Shared victories are when teams equal on match points to share the championship.

France

France's national team, known as Les Bleus, played in the tournament for the first time in 1910. This was the year that the Home Nations became the Five Nations. They have since won the trophy on 25 (eight shared) occasions.

Wales

Holding the second-most outright tournament wins, Wales have achieved a Grand Slam (when a team beats all of the others in the competition) in 12 of their 39 championship victories. England are top with 13.

SIX NATIONS

The Six Nations Championship is a tournament held in February and March every year. England, Ireland, Wales, Scotland, France, and Italy all compete to lift the trophy. It's the most important competition for these nations after the World Cup. The Six Nations succeeded the Home and Five Nations Championships.

HOW IT STARTED...

The tournament started as a four-team Home Nations Championship (England, Ireland, Scotland, and Wales) in 1883.

 Scotland

Sometimes called The Thistle, Scotland are original tournament members with England, Wales, and Ireland. They've lifted the cup 24 times (nine shared), and three of these were Grand Slam victories. They also won the last Five Nations in 1999.

Ireland

Ireland won the Six Nations in 2014, 2015, and 2018 (Grand Slam) and have been champions 23 times in all (nine shared). They won the tournament outright for the first time in 1894. They were second in the world rankings at the start of 2019.

Italy

The tournament's newest addition is Italy, who joined in 2000 and made it the Six Nations. They won their first game against reigning champions Scotland. However, the "Azzurri" have yet to win the competition.

Figures for Six Nations are correct as of 18 March 2019.

ONES TO WATCH

The 2019 World Cup in Japan will feature the best players competing for the biggest prize in rugby. Here are some of the star names in the tournament.

 **Jonathan Davies**

This brilliant Welsh centre is a key player for his country. A World Cup semi-finalist in 2011, Davies will be keen to make up for missing the 2015 tournament due to injury.

TEAM	Wales
POSITION	Centre
YEARS	2011
BORN	April 5, 1988
FROM	Solihull, England

 ## Stuart Hogg

The full-back impressed at the 2015 World Cup where Scotland reached the quarter-finals. Expect even more from him when he plays in Japan with his much-improved team.

TEAM	Scotland
POSITION	Full-back
YEARS	2015
BORN	June 24, 1992
FROM	Melrose, Scotland

 ## Sergio Parisse

Italy's captain and most-capped player is one of rugby's greatest number 8s. At the age of 36, it could be his last World Cup, so he'll want to make it one to remember!

TEAM	Italy
POSITION	Number 8
YEARS	2003, 2007, 2011, 2015
BORN	September 12, 1983
FROM	La Plata, Argentina

 **Beauden Barrett**

Barrett is one of the best players on the planet. This two-time World Rugby Player of the Year scored the last try in New Zealand's 34–17 victory in the 2015 World Cup final against Australia.

TEAM	New Zealand
POSITION	Fly-half
YEARS	2015
BORN	May 27, 1991
FROM	New Plymouth, New Zealand

Kenki Fukuoka

This wing made his Japan debut against the Philippines in 2013. He was part of the 2015 World Cup squad that won three of their four matches.

TEAM	Japan
POSITION	Wing
YEARS	2015
BORN	September 7, 1992
FROM	Fukuoka, Japan

Teddy Thomas

This wing scored a hat-trick of tries on his France debut. Thomas will want to prove his talent on the biggest stage after being left out of Les Bleus' 2015 World Cup squad.

TEAM	France
POSITION	Wing
YEARS	N/A
BORN	September 18, 1993
FROM	Biarritz, France

Israel Folau

The superstar full-back has been named the Australian Wallabies' Player of the Year a record three times! Folau helped Australia finish as runners-up at the 2015 World Cup.

TEAM	Australia
POSITION	Full-back
YEARS	2015
BORN	April 3, 1989
FROM	Minto, Australia

Nicolás Sánchez

Sánchez is a pinpoint-accurate fly-half on Argentina's men's team, the Pumas. He was top scorer at the 2015 World Cup with 97 points and scored 20 penalties to help Argentina finish fourth.

TEAM	Argentina
POSITION	Fly-half
YEARS	2011, 2015
BORN	October 26, 1988
FROM	San Miguel de Tucumán, Argentina

Owen Farrell

Farrell is the second-highest England points-scorer ever. He had a disappointing 2015 World Cup when England failed to reach the knockout stage for the first time. The captain will be aiming for better at the 2019 tournament.

TEAM	England
POSITION	Fly-half
YEARS	2015
BORN	September 24, 1991
FROM	Billinge, England

Siya Kolisi

Kolisi will captain South Africa in Japan 2019. After playing just 34 minutes of the 2015 tournament, he will be determined to lead the Springboks to glory. South Africa last won the Rugby World Cup back in 1995.

TEAM	South Africa
POSITION	Flanker
YEARS	2015
BORN	June 16, 1991
FROM	Zwide, South Africa

Bundee Aki

This centre is one of Ireland's top players. He was a big part of their 2018 Six Nations Grand Slam win, even though his debut was only four months before.

TEAM	Ireland
POSITION	Centre
YEARS	N/A
BORN	April 7, 1990
FROM	Auckland, New Zealand

Sonatane Takulua

This scrum-half played at the 2015 tournament. He will be a top pick for Tonga's team. He scored the most points at the 2017 Pacific Nations Cup with 25 points to his name.

TEAM	Tonga
POSITION	Scrum-half
YEARS	2015
BORN	January 11, 1991
FROM	Lapaha, Tonga

LEGENDARY TEAMS

These incredible sides have secured their place in the history books for their standout performances at rugby union's biggest tournament.

FRANCE MEN, 2011

France overcame the odds in the knockout rounds to achieve shock wins against England and then Wales. They reached the final, where they narrowly lost 8-7 to hosts and favourites, New Zealand.

SOUTH AFRICA MEN, 1995

In the Springboks' first ever World Cup appearance, the team rose to the pressure of playing in their home country. They beat New Zealand in extra time in the final to win the Webb Ellis Cup.

NEW ZEALAND MEN, 2011–2015

After winning the World Cup on home soil in 2011, the All Blacks became the first team to successfully defend the trophy in 2015.

AUSTRALIA MEN, 1999

The Wallabies became the first team to win a World Cup held in rugby union's professional era (from 1995). They beat France in the final at Cardiff's Millennium Stadium.

NEW ZEALAND WOMEN, 1998–2010

The Black Ferns dominated the women's World Cup for 12 years. They won four successive tournaments from 1998, winning all 19 matches they played.

USA WOMEN, 1991

The American team of 1991 conceded just six points on their way to lifting the first women's World Cup in Wales. They defeated England 19-6 in the final at Cardiff Arms Park in front of almost 3,000 fans.

ENGLAND MEN, 2003

England's first World Cup final victory was secured when they defeated Australia in Sydney. England beat South Africa, Wales, and France on the way to the final.

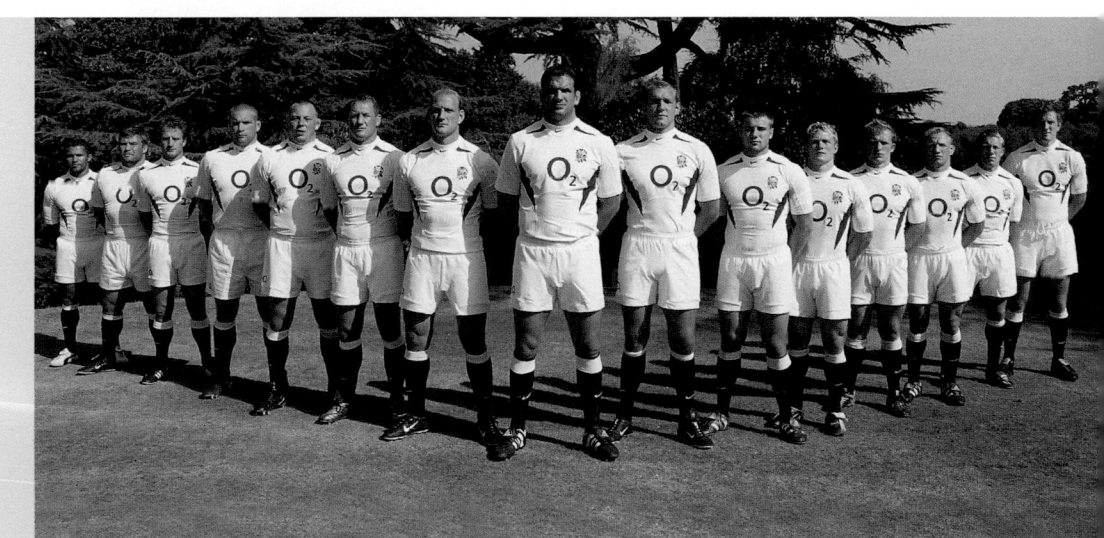

LEGENDARY GAMES

Some rugby games are especially high on drama and tension. Let's take a moment to look at some of the epic matches from rugby history that fans around the world will never forget.

JAPAN MEN 34–32 SOUTH AFRICA MEN, 2015

The Cherry Blossoms caused probably the biggest upset in World Cup history when they stunned two-time winners South Africa. Karne Hesketh scored the winning try in the last minute of extra time!

NEW ZEALAND WOMEN 25–17 ENGLAND WOMEN, 2006

New Zealand faced England in the finals. With an epic performance from fly-half Anna Richards, they won their third World Cup in a row.

AUSTRALIA MEN 17–20 ENGLAND MEN, 2003

This close final in Sydney could have been won by either team. Australia fought hard, with Lote Tuqiri scoring a try just six minutes in. However, Jonny Wilkinson's drop goal in extra time saw England take the trophy away from the hosts and holders.

FRANCE MEN 20–18 NEW ZEALAND MEN, 2007

In the 2007 quarter-finals, France went from 13-3 down at half-time, to beating New Zealand, who were among the tournament favourites. Yannick Jauzion scored the match-winning try for France.

CANADA WOMEN 18–16 FRANCE WOMEN, 2014

Hosts France were on the end of a shock defeat as Canada held off a late fightback from Les Bleues. Wing Magali Harvey scored the try of the match, taking Canada to the final for the first time.

WESTERN SAMOA MEN 16–13 WALES MEN, 1991

After years of predictable winners, Western Samoa became the first non-seeded team to beat a seeded nation. They defeated Wales on home soil in their first World Cup match.

SOUTH AFRICA MEN 15–12 NEW ZEALAND MEN, 1995

This match was so legendary that it was made into a film (*Invictus*) starring Matt Damon. South Africa's incredible World Cup win helped to unite a nation divided by apartheid.

WINNERS' ROLL

Lots of teams battle for glory but only one can come out on top. Let's take a look at the past tournament champions, highest scorers, and World Cup winners!

SIX NATIONS WINNERS (MEN)

YEAR	WINNER
2000	England
2001	England
2002	France *(Grand Slam)*
2003	England *(Grand Slam)*
2004	France *(Grand Slam)*
2005	Wales *(Grand Slam)*
2006	France
2007	France
2008	Wales *(Grand Slam)*
2009	Ireland *(Grand Slam)*
2010	France *(Grand Slam)*
2011	England
2012	Wales *(Grand Slam)*
2013	Wales
2014	Ireland
2015	Ireland
2016	England *(Grand Slam)*
2017	England
2018	Ireland *(Grand Slam)*
2019	Wales *(Grand Slam)*

SIX NATIONS WINNERS (WOMEN)

YEAR	WINNER
2002	France *(Grand Slam)*
2003	England *(Grand Slam)*
2004	France *(Grand Slam)*
2005	France *(Grand Slam)*
2006	England *(Grand Slam)*
2007	England *(Grand Slam)*
2008	England *(Grand Slam)*
2009	England
2010	England *(Grand Slam)*
2011	England *(Grand Slam)*
2012	England *(Grand Slam)*
2013	Ireland *(Grand Slam)*
2014	France *(Grand Slam)*
2015	Ireland
2016	France
2017	England *(Grand Slam)*
2018	France *(Grand Slam)*

SIX NATIONS TOP 6 HIGH POINTS SCORERS OF ALL TIME (MEN)*

1. Ronan O'Gara *(Ireland)* 557
2. Jonny Wilkinson *(England)* 546
3. Stephen Jones *(Wales)* 467
4. Neil Jenkins *(Wales)* 406
5. Chris Paterson *(Scotland)* 403
6. Owen Farrell *(England)* 402

There isn't official data for the equivalent female scorers available.

High scorers as on 18 March 2019

RUGBY UNION

WORLD CUP WINNERS (MEN)

NEW ZEALAND	**3 WINS**	*(1987, 2011, 2015)*
AUSTRALIA	**2 WINS**	*(1991, 1999)*
SOUTH AFRICA	**2 WINS**	*(1995, 2007)*
ENGLAND	**1 WIN**	*(2003)*

WORLD CUP TOP 3 POINTS SCORERS OF ALL TIME (MEN)

1. Jonny Wilkinson *(England)*.......................... **277**
2. Gavin Hastings *(Scotland)*.......................... **227**
3. Michael Lynagh *(Australia)* **195**

WORLD CUP WINNERS (WOMEN)

YEAR	WINNER	SCORE	RUNNER UP
1991	United States	19-6	England
1994	England	38-23	United States
1998	New Zealand	44-12	United States
2002	New Zealand	19-9	England
2006	New Zealand	25-17	England
2010	New Zealand	13-10	England
2014	England	21-9	Canada
2017	New Zealand	41-32	England

WORLD CUP TOP 3 TRY SCORERS OF ALL TIME (WOMEN)

1. Portia Woodman *(New Zealand)* **13**
2. Elissa Alarie *(Canada)*.......................... **6**
3. Magali Harvey *(Canada)* **6**

RUGBY LEAGUE

WORLD CUP WINNERS (MEN)

AUSTRALIA	**11 WINS**	*(1957, 1968, 1970, 1975, 1977, 1985-88, 1989-92, 1995, 2000, 2013, 2017)*
GREAT BRITAIN	**3 WINS**	*(1954, 1960, 1972)*
NEW ZEALAND	**1 WIN**	*(2008)*

WORLD CUP TOP 3 POINTS SCORERS OF ALL TIME (MEN)

1. Johnathan Thurston *(Australia)*................. **124**
2. Mick Cronin *(Australia)*.......................... **112**
3. Michael O'Connor *(Australia)*...................... **108**

WORLD CUP WINNERS (WOMEN)

YEAR	WINNER	SCORE	RUNNER UP
2000	New Zealand	26-4	Great Britain
2005	New Zealand	58-0	New Zealand Maori
2008	New Zealand	34-0	Australia
2013	Australia	22-12	New Zealand
2017	Australia	23-16	New Zealand

WORLD CUP TOP 3 TRY SCORERS (WOMEN) *from the 2017 World Cup*

1. Honey Hireme *(New Zealand)*...................... **13**
2. Karina Brown *(Australia)*.......................... **6**
3. Isabelle Kelly *(Australia)*.......................... **6**

High scorers as on 1 January 2019

GLOSSARY

apartheid Historical system of separating people by race, particularly used in South Africa in the past

backs Group of players numbered 9 to 15 who do not participate in scrums and lineouts, except for the scrum-half

beach rugby Version of rugby played on sand with four or seven players on each side

cap When a player represents their country in an international match

contact rugby When touching and tackling an opponent is allowed

conversion Kick between the posts after being awarded a try for an extra two points

drop goal Kick between the posts by an attacking side that scores three points. The ball must hit the ground before being kicked.

forward pass Illegal pass where the ball goes forwards

forwards Group of players numbered 1 to 8 who bind together into scrums, line up for lineouts, and take part in rucks and mauls

foul When a player or team breaks a rule

free kick Kick awarded to a team, usually because a minor rule has been broken by the other team

front row Name for the props and hooker combination at the front of a scrum

goal line Line across each end of the pitch past which players must touch the ball to the ground to score a try

Grand Slam Six Nations championship won without any losses or draws

high ball Ball kicked very high into the air

injury time Time referee adds on at the end of the half to make up for stopping and starting playing time for interruptions

knock on Losing, dropping, or knocking the ball forward from a player's hand

League Version of rugby played with 13 players per team with different rules to union

lineout Way of re-starting play after the ball has been taken out or kicked to touch

loose forward Common names for the flankers and number 8 in a forward pack

maul When at least three players from either side clump together, challenging the player with the ball

mini rugby Version of rugby played with a smaller ball on a smaller pitch

most capped Player who has played the most games for their country

non-contact rugby When contact with an opponent is not allowed

non-tackle rugby When tackling an opponent is not allowed

offsides During scrums, lineouts, and mauls an imaginary line is present. If any player crosses this before the play is completed, they commit a foul.

Pacific Nations Cup Annual tournament between the national men's teams of Fiji, Samoa, and Tonga

penalty Opportunity to advance or score awarded to a team after the other team breaks a rule

penalty kick Kicks awarded to a team when the other team breaks a major rule

pitch Playing surface that a game is played on

Pumas National rugby union team of Argentina

red card Card the referee shows a player to send them off for the rest of the game

referee Match official responsible for enforcing the laws of the game

ruck When one or more players from each team close around the ball to obtain possession after a player is tackled

Rugby Football Union (RFU) Governing body for rugby union in England

Rugby World Cup (RWC) International rugby union tournament played every four years. League equivalent is the Rugby League World Cup.

scrum Contest for the ball involving eight players from each team. The players bind together and push against the opposition.

scrum-half Back wearing number 9 who normally feeds the ball into a scrum. The player retrieves the ball from scrums, rucks, and mauls

sevens Form of rugby union played with only seven players on each team

sin bin Where players who have received yellow cards sit for 10 minutes

Six Nations Annual tournament between the national men's and women's teams of England, Wales, Ireland, Scotland, France, and Italy

snow rugby Version of rugby played in deep snow between two teams of seven players

tag rugby Non-contact version of rugby. Each team has five to seven players who wear two tags on their shorts.

tap penalty Type of penalty taken quickly, where a player taps the ball with their foot and catches it

tens rugby Form of rugby union played with only ten players on each team

touch rugby Non-tackle version of rugby with six players on each team

touchline Out-of-bounds line that runs on either side of the pitch

try Score of five points awarded when the ball is grounded across the goal line

Union Most popular form of rugby, with 15 players on each team

Webb Ellis Cup Trophy awarded to the winners of the Rugby World Cup

wheelchair rugby Version of rugby for players who have a physical disability that requires the use of a wheelchair

World Rugby Worldwide governing body for rugby union

yellow card Card the referee shows a player to send them off for 10 minutes. The player leaves the pitch and sits in the sin bin.

INDEX

ACKNOWLEDGEMENTS

The publisher would like to thank the following people for their assistance: Sally Beets, Katie Lawrence, Abi Luscombe, and Seeta Parmar for editorial assistance; Romi Chakraborty for design management.

The publisher would like to thank the following for their kind permission to reproduce their photographs:

(Key: a-above; b-below/bottom; c-centre; f-far; l-left; r-right; t-top)

1 123RF.com: Wavebreak Media Ltd (c/Ball, c/Stadium). **2 Getty Images:** David Rogers (bc); Tony Marshall / Stringer (br). **4-5 Alamy Stock Photo:** robertharding / Godong. **5 Dreamstime.com:** Magdalena Żurawska (cla). **6-7 Getty Images:** Warren Little. **7 Alamy Stock Photo:** Paul Cunningham (tr); John Fryer (cl); Oscar Max (crb). **8 Alamy Stock Photo:** Granger Historical Picture Archive (cra). **Getty Images:** Popperfoto / Contributor (bc). **9 Getty Images:** Shaun Botterill (cra). **10-11 Alamy Stock Photo:** Paul Cunningham (c). **11 Getty Images:** Mark Kolbe (r). **12-13 Getty Images:** Zak Kaczmarek / Stringer (t). **12 Alamy Stock Photo:** Zefrog (bl). **13 Alamy Stock Photo:** Jonathan Larsen / Diadem Images (bl). **Getty Images:** Chet Strange / AFP (br). **14 Alamy Stock Photo:** RichSTOCK. **15 Alamy Stock Photo:** Kevin Britland (clb). **Rex by Shutterstock:** Juice (cra). **16 Rex by Shutterstock:** Tom Dwyer / Seconds Left. **19 Alamy Stock Photo:** Action Plus Sports Images (bl); Massimiliano Carnabuci (cra). **20 Getty Images:** Tony Marshall / Stringer. **21 Getty Images:** David Rogers (cla); Martin Hunter / Stringer (br). **22 Getty Images:** Alex Livesey. **23 Getty Images:** Stu Forster. **24 Getty Images:** Mike Hewitt (cla); David Rogers (br). **25 Getty Images:** Mark Kolbe. **26 Getty Images:** Simon Bruty / Allsport. **27 Rex by Shutterstock:** (cla); Michael Paler (br). **28 Getty Images:** Christian Liewig - Corbis / Contributor. **30 Getty Images:** Bradley Kanaris (cla). **31 Alamy Stock Photo:** Stephen Bisgrove (tr). **32 Alamy Stock Photo:** Elsie Kibue / EK13 Photos (cla). **33 Getty Images:** Adrian Dennis / AFP (cr). **34 Alamy Stock Photo:** Elsie Kibue / EK13 Photos (cla). **Getty Images:** Mike Brett / Popperfoto / Contributor (bc). **35 Getty Images:** Mitchell Gunn / Contributor (crb). **36 Getty Images:** Jean Paul Thomas / Thomas Pictures / Icon Sport. **37 Getty Images:** Dave Rogers / Allsport (cla); Michael Bradley (br). **38-39 Getty Images:** Eddy Lemaistre / Corbis. **40-41 Getty Images:** David Rogers. **43 Getty Images:** Christophe Simon / AFP (cra); Ken Ishii (crb). **44-45 Alamy Stock Photo:** Paul Cunningham. **46 Getty Images:** Ian MacNicol / Stringer. **47 Getty Images:** Gareth Copley (br); Richard Heathcote (cla). **48 Getty Images:** McCarthy / Sportsfile. **49 Getty Images:** David Rogers (clb); The Asahi Shimbun (cra). **50 Getty Images:** Stu Forster (br); Matt King / Stringer (cla). **51 Getty Images:** David Rogers. **52 Getty Images:** Chris Hyde / Stringer. **53 Getty Images:** Scott Barbour (bl); Phil Walter (cra). **54 Alamy Stock Photo:** Action Plus Sports Images. **55 Alamy Stock Photo:** f8 archive (cr). **Getty Images:** David Rogers (b). **56 Getty Images:** David Rogers (cr). **57 Getty Images:** Christian Liewig - Corbis / Contributor (cra, cl). **64 Alamy Stock Photo:** Action Plus Sports Images (b)

Cover images: *Front and Back:* **Dreamstime.com:** Kirsty Pargeter / Kj; *Front:* **123RF.com:** Wavebreak Media Ltd c/ (Ball), c/ (Stadium); **Alamy Stock Photo:** PCN Photography crb; **Dreamstime.com:** Wavebreakmedia Ltd fcrb; **Getty Images:** John Gichigi / Staff clb; **iStockphoto.com:** peepo / E+ fclb; *Back:* **Dreamstime.com:** Jorge Salcedo / Jorgeantonio (Background); **iStockphoto.com:** peepo / E+ (Players); *Spine:* **iStockphoto.com:** peepo / E+ t

All other images © Dorling Kindersley
For further information see: www.dkimages.com

New Zealand celebrating their 2015 World Cup win

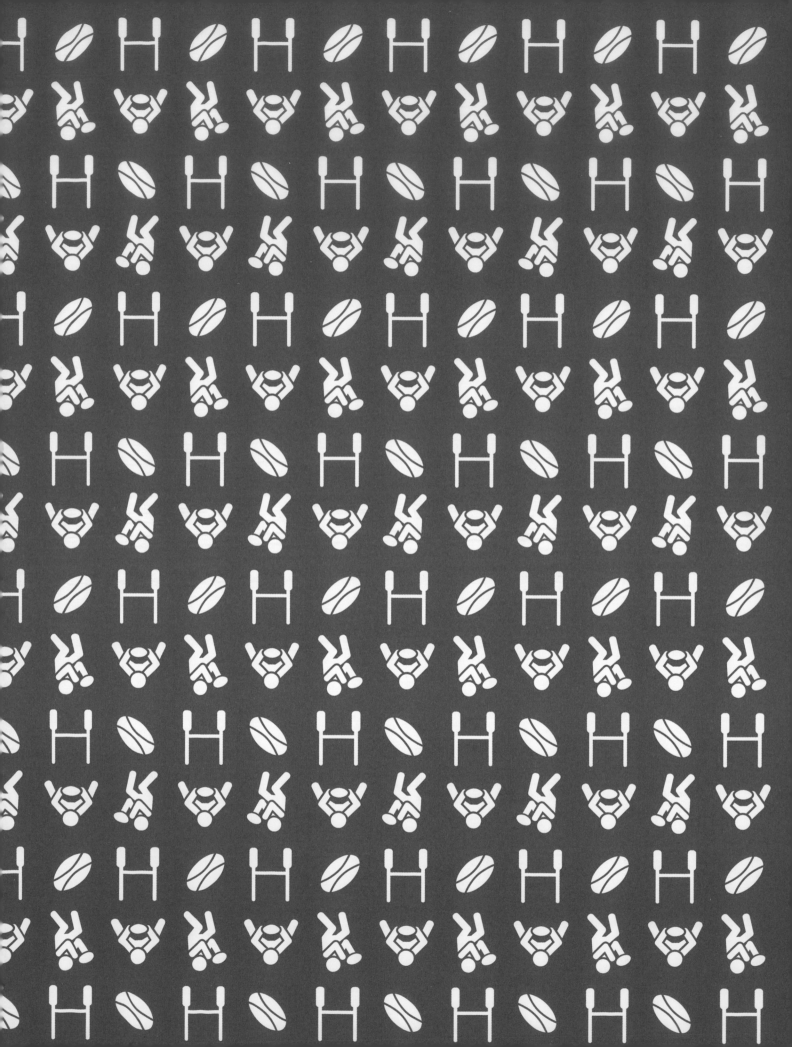